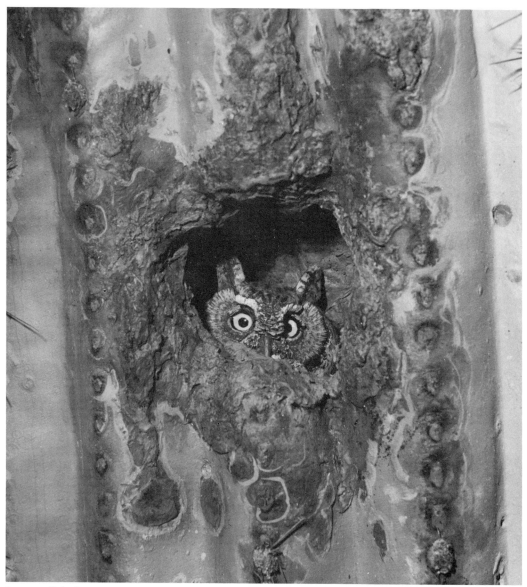

Laurence Pringle

Laurence Pringle

How Animals Find Comfort and Safety

Charles Scribner's Sons · New York

Charles Scribner's Sons Books for Young Readers
Macmillan Publishing Company
866 Third Avenue, New York, NY 10022
Collier Macmillan Canada, Inc.

Printed in the United States of America
First Edition
10 9 8 7 6 5 4 3 2 1

Library of Congress Cataloging-in-Publication Data
Pringle, Laurence P.
  Home: how animals find comfort and safety.
  Bibliography: p.
  Includes index.
  Summary: Examines the characteristics of the many different types of places in which animals make their home.
  1. Animals—Habitations—Juvenile literature.
  [1. Animals—Habitations] I. Title.
QL756.P75 1987   591.56'4   87-13119
ISBN 0-684-18526-1

Contents

About This Book

The planet earth is home for millions of different kinds of animals. Many of them are tropical insects that scientists have not yet named or described. All of these animals, from giant whales to tiny ants, have homes of some sort.

A home may be a safe refuge for most of an animal's life or one of several that it uses over its life-span. Some animal homes are complex structures; others are just a space an animal occupies temporarily or a territory an animal knows and defends. An animal's home can also be its food-catching device, or one animal can make its home and get its food on the outside or even the inside of another creature. The possibilities are as great as the extraordinary variety of life on earth.

The need for safety and comfort is so basic that the study of an animal's home leads inevitably to knowledge about its relationships with other things, living and nonliving, in its environment. This is a definition of ecology—a term that comes from the

HOME

Greek words *oikos* ("home") and *logos* ("study"). Home is a simple, plain word, but the study of animal homes can lead in fascinating directions and to exciting discoveries.

This book concentrates on the homes of animals found in North America and tells about some creatures you may find in your own back yard and neighborhood or in a nearby park. It reveals something about how the homes are made and used and how vital a home is to all living things.

1 A Hole in the Ground

One of the most basic, down-to-earth kinds of homes is a hole in the ground. Some animals find shelter in natural hollows, others in burrows dug by themselves or by other species. Biologists have used everything from trowels to large backhoe machines to excavate animal burrows and learn about the lives of such hole-diggers as fiddler crabs and prairie dogs.

One animal that seems safe from such direct probing is a species of tilefish that lives along the Atlantic seaboard. Tilefish grow up to three feet in length. Most of them live along the edge of the outer continental shelf where the water is between four hundred and nine hundred feet deep. There tilefish find the year-round water temperature they need—between 48° and 57° F. And there in the ocean floor and in the walls of underwater canyons they dig their burrows.

Biologists have observed tilefish from small research submarines and first saw their burrows in 1977. The fish seem able to dig

1

vertical holes by moving their pectoral fins, creating currents that push soft sediments aside. In order to tunnel horizontally into clay canyon walls, they probably dig with their mouths. When a submarine came close, the fish fled headfirst into these shelters and later emerged tailfirst—evidence that their burrows are probably simple shafts with no space for turning around.

Tilefish may stay in or near their burrows except when hunting for crabs, a favorite food. Tilefish themselves are preyed upon by sharks. In fact, shark predation may have caused tilefish to become

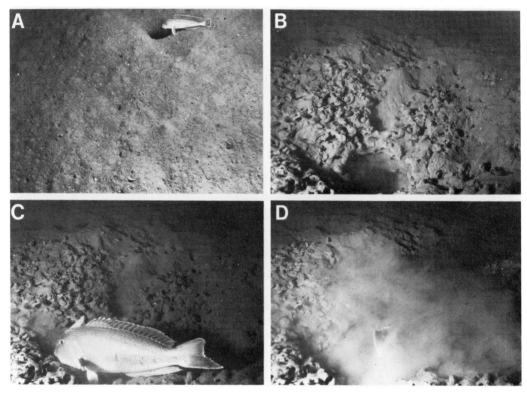

Kenneth W. Able

Tilefish dig burrows hundreds of feet beneath the ocean surface. Photo A shows a one-foot-long juvenile tilefish by its burrow. Photos B-D show the burrow entrance of a three-foot-long tilefish, which stirs up sediment (Photo D) when it swims into its burrow.

burrowers. Now their diggings mark thousands of square miles of the ocean floor and also provide shelter for smaller fish, eels, lobsters, and crabs.

Any shelter dug by one animal may be used later by other species. Once a groundhog digs its underground home, the system of entrances, tunnels, and chambers may be used by generations of woodchucks to come and by skunks, opossums, rabbits, and—after enlargement—by foxes.

Nowhere is belowground shelter more sought after than in prairies and deserts. Prey animals need hideouts from hawks and coyotes; they also seek respite from searing summer heat. So the diggings of prairie dogs are also homes for cottontail rabbits, jackrabbits, lizards, snakes, burrowing owls, and insects.

Prairie dogs are plump, short-eared rodents that live only in the North American Great Plains. They once numbered in the billions. A Texas prairie dog colony, reported by biologist C. Hart Merriam in 1901, covered an estimated 25,000 square miles. Merriam claimed that 400 million prairie dogs lived there. Throughout their range these rodents were considered pests by farmers and ranchers, who killed many of them with poisons. Today the destruction of their habitat reduces their numbers further. They are still found in a dozen states, and in small areas of Canada and Mexico.

Early in this century, employees of the United States Department of Agriculture actually dug with pick and shovel to uncover the secrets of prairie dog burrows. Today prairie dogs are appreciated by many people, in part because of our knowledge about the engineering of their underground homes.

Of four species, the black-tailed prairie dog is the most common resident of flat plains. It piles mounds of soil around its two burrow entrances; the mounded earth prevents rainwater from flooding its home. One mound is low and broad. The other rises to

A prairie dog feeds near its burrow, ready to dash to safety underground. Snakes, lizards, and burrowing owls also hide in prairie dog homes.

three feet in the air and looks like a volcanic crater. Below this high mound the tunnel shaft plunges straight down as far as fourteen feet before turning horizontal. Just a few feet down, however, a prairie dog clears a side chamber, which is called the listening room. When a prairie dog flees from a coyote, human, or other potential enemy, it usually stops in the listening room. There it scolds the intruder and listens for clues that danger has passed.

A prairie dog burrow may include more than a hundred feet of tunnels, with several side chambers. The deepest is a grass-lined nursery where young are born and nursed. Others serve as food storage chambers or toilets. A toilet chamber may be used for a while, then sealed off with a plug of soil. Many species of burrowing mammals have similar "sanitation systems" in their homes.

The microclimate within a prairie dog home is often dramatically different from conditions aboveground. Year around the burrow air is moister, and stored food absorbs moisture from the air. So the food of prairie dogs gives them some water, so precious on the semiarid plains. The burrow temperature is also more moderate than aboveground—cooler in summer, warmer in winter. (This is also true of the desert burrows of kangaroo rats of the Southwest, of the similar jerboas of North African deserts, and of wild gerbils of West Africa.)

A prairie dog burrow has a sort of air-conditioning system—the result of the different elevations and structures of the two entrances. Air tends to flow into the low mound and out of the high, chimney-like mound. When investigators dropped lighted candles into burrows, smoke rose only from the tall mound. Air currents bring oxygen to the deepest tunnels and chambers and carry off waste carbon dioxide.

No wonder that many animals seek the hospitable shelter of abandoned or even occupied prairie dog burrows. It is not true, however, that such creatures as rattlesnakes and burrowing owls live in harmony with prairie dogs in their homes. The casual observer, seeing only aboveground, may think that these animals tolerate the presence of one another. But belowground, both the owls and snakes are known to kill and eat young prairie dogs. And, given the chance, prairie dogs eat the eggs and young of burrowing owls.

HOME

Far from the dry plains, at the edge of the sea, live other burrow-diggers—fiddler crabs. They dig their homes in the mud or sand of saltwater marshes and live in them in all seasons. Fiddler crabs emerge to feed when the tide goes out, then retreat underground when the tide returns.

Fiddlers are named for the appearance and behavior of the male crabs. They have one exceptionally large claw and wave it about rhythmically, somewhat like a fiddle-player. When a female is attracted, she and the male retreat to his burrow and mate. Rival males rush at one another, shoving and grabbing, but seldom hurt one another. At the slightest hint of danger, all fiddler crabs scuttle to their homes.

An incoming tide also sends the crabs below, but different species of fiddlers respond in different ways. One called *Uca pugilator* digs its burrows in sandy creek banks. If *pugilator* fails to reach its burrow in time, rising water causes the sand walls to collapse. Its refuge gone, the crab is in danger of being eaten by fish that come hunting with the tide.

These fiddlers usually avoid this fate by entering their burrows more and more frequently as high tide approaches. As soon as rising water wets the bottom of their burrows, *pugilator* crabs pull sand into the entrance and pack it into a plug. This traps some air in the burrow, and the air supports the walls of the crab's home as the tide inundates the surface above.

Another fiddler crab, *Uca pugnax,* has an easier time of it because it digs in mud. The tunnels of *pugnax* crabs, as much as three feet deep, do not collapse or need to be plugged at high tide. These fiddlers often stay aboveground until water laps at their feet, then scurry to the safety of their homes.

Many animals build shelters not for themselves but for their young. Female digger wasps, for example, make a simple nest cavity for each egg they lay and stock it with a food supply. After

6

Fiddler crab burrows dug in mud may reach three feet beneath the surface. The crabs may feed aboveground until the waters of high tide lap at their feet.

digging a burrow in the soil, a female wasp stings a caterpillar, grasshopper, or other prey, then carries the paralyzed insect to the burrow and drags it in. She lays an egg on the still-living prey, which is eaten later by the larva that hatches from the egg.

Digger wasps eventually seal the openings of these nests. Some species hunt for a pebble of just the right size with which to plug the opening. And some also pick up a stone, shell, or other hard object in their mouths and pound down the soil that fills the top of the burrow. They bring more loose soil, again pick up their stone tool, and hammer the soil down until the nest hole resembles the surrounding soil surface. Certain soil conditions stimulate this behavior in digger wasps. Their use of a tool does not demonstrate human-like problem solving, but digger wasps are remarkable enough in their own wasp-like way.

2 Catching Food at Home

Many animals must leave the shelter of home to seek food. For some, however, home itself is a food-catching device. About fifteen thousand kinds of spiders rely on their webs to trap food. They have poor eyesight, but their webs serve as extensions of their sense of touch. Vibrations tell them where in the web an insect is caught and how big it is.

All spiders release silk from organs called spinnerets, located on the tip of their abdomens. Each of the web-spinning species makes a web of distinctive design, ranging from careless-looking tangles to precise, symmetrical structures. They include sheets, hammocks, domes, funnels, tubes, and wheel-shaped orbs.

People find the design of orb webs especially appealing, and both professional scientists and amateur naturalists have observed the behavior of the orb builders. The webs we see are almost always the work of adult females; males stop spinning when they are quite young.

Orb webs are well-designed to catch flying insects. A female spider spins its web at night, then rests in or near it and waits for food to be trapped.

Each orb weaver begins by laying down a horizontal bridge thread that becomes the uppermost support of her web. Then she usually walks back and forth, strengthening the bridge by adding more silk. From the bridge and from vertical side threads the spider establishes several radii—foundation lines that will be the "spokes" of the wheel-shaped web.

The hub, where all of the spokes meet, may be strengthened before the spider begins the next stage. Starting at the hub, she works outward, laying down silk in a loosely spaced spiral. This serves as scaffolding for the last step. Starting near the outer edge of her web, the spider retraces her path, eating the scaffolding lines as she moves in a spiral toward the hub, spinning out new lines of sticky silk. These insect-trapping lines are more numerous and more closely spaced than the scaffolding. (The webs of some orb weavers have dry, fuzzy capture threads, not sticky ones, that entangle prey.)

Most orb weavers rebuild their webs every night. They eat the spiral of sticky threads and replace or reinforce any damaged lines of the frame and radii. Then a new sticky spiral is spun. This predawn process takes about a half hour.

The spider rests at the hub or at the edge of the web, perhaps inside a partly rolled-up leaf. She always stays in touch with one or more radii of her web, awaiting vibrations that signal captured prey. The struggles of a large and dangerous bee are ignored, or the spider approaches cautiously and cuts the lines around this catch, letting it drop out of the web. The more delicate vibrations from an edible fly bring the spider on the run. Stepping only on dry threads, she reaches her prey, bites it, and wraps it in silk, or first wraps it, then delivers a poisonous bite. Usually the spider carries the prey to her retreat before eating.

Scientists have found that orb-web spiders spin their webs with great efficiency, wasting little material or energy. An orb web sets an insect trap across a large area with a small amount of silk. While maintaining her web a spider recycles nearly all of her silk. After being eaten it emerges from her spinnerets as new silk within twenty-four hours. And, according to one spider researcher, the food energy from about half a fly "pays the expenses" of daily web building.

Another example of energy-saving behavior by certain orb makers was reported in 1983. Biologists had long been puzzled by bands or patches of white silk they found in some orb webs. These markings did not seem to be of any use in catching prey, nor did they seem to protect spiders from predators. Then Cornell University biologist Thomas Eisner noticed that birds flying toward such orb webs would often see them in time and veer away. He also remembered that the only orb weavers that include white markings are those that leave their webs up in the daytime, when most birds are active.

This suggested to Eisner that the markings might be warning signs to birds and other large animals that might tear through webs. Experiments confirmed that birds do collide with unmarked webs much more often than they do with webs with warning patches. Of course the markings may also cause some flying insects to veer off, but the spiders still gain by having their webs up longer and by not needing to rebuild entire webs that have been ripped away by a passing bird.

Spider webs are a familiar sight to almost everyone, but few people have ever seen the food-trap-homes of insects called caddis flies. The larvae of these insects occur almost worldwide in rivers and streams. Dozens of species weave silken webs underwater. The silk forms in their mouths when two liquids are released simultaneously from saliva glands. The webs, or nets, of various species are shaped like trumpets, sausages, funnels, or sacks. The biggest are four inches long and two inches wide, although some

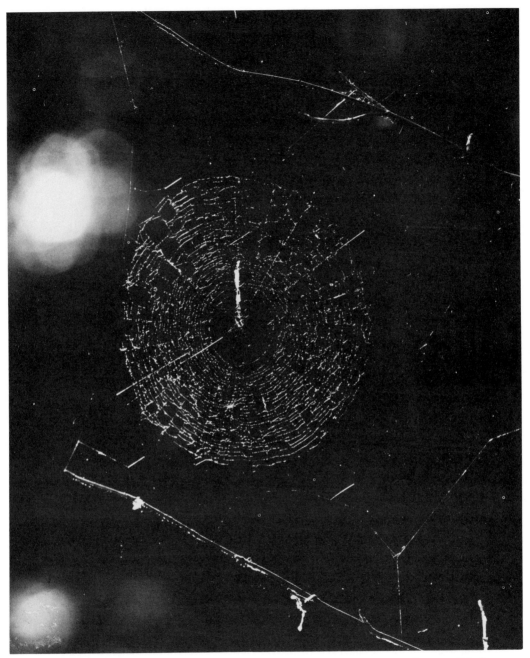

Laurence Pringle

A patch of white silk in an orb web seems to serve as a warning to birds that ordinarily might fly through the web and destroy it.

slender trumpet-shaped nets reach eight inches in length. Most are much smaller and are easily missed when you look for them from the bank of a stream.

Some caddis fly nets are spun at the brink of miniature waterfalls, yet they seem as delicate as finely woven spider webs. Most are set between two stones or other objects on the stream bottom, placed at right angles to the current. The nets act as filters, trapping bits of food, including live insects, from water flowing downstream. The net spinners lurk nearby or in part of the net itself. Some larvae are grazing animals that clean tiny food particles, including bacteria, from their net. Others are meat-eaters and rush out like spiders to attack their live prey.

Biologists have found that the largest species of net-spinning caddis fly larvae live in streams that carry small amounts of food particles. They build large nets in places where the current is fastest. This ensures that great volumes of water pass through the net. In streams where drifting food is abundant, net-spinning caddis flies tend to be small. They build smaller nets and set them in places where the current is slower. With plenty of food in the water, they do not need to filter large amounts of water in order to get all they need.

Another sort of insect larva, living on dry land, also sets a trap for its food. This predator of other insects is so remarkable that its name—ant lion—is also applied to its adult stage, a delicate flying insect that resembles a damselfly. Adult female ant lions lay eggs in sand or loose, dry soil. The larvae that hatch are the real ant lions—squat, wedge-shaped predatory creatures with pincer-like mandibles.

Soon after hatching, an ant lion digs its first funnel-shaped pit in the sand. It digs by moving backward, plowing with its abdomen and flicking sand upward with its head. Then the ant lion lies motionless just beneath the surface at the bottom of the pit, waiting for food to arrive.

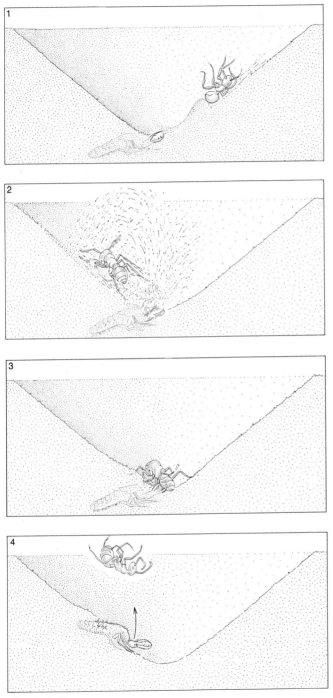

An ant tumbles down the slope of an antlion's pit, toward the sharp mandibles of the antlion (1). When prey begins to escape, the antlion flicks sand with its head (2), sometimes knocking the ant close enough to grasp (3). After sucking fluids from its prey, the antlion flicks the dry carcass out of the pit (4).

Alan D. Iselin

HOME

That food can be any animal small enough to slip down into the little pit. Ants are common prey, but spiders, beetles, caterpillars, and sow bugs may also pass within reach of an ant lion's jaws. If the ant lion fails to grab its prey and the animal tries to scramble up the slope of the pit, the ant lion flicks sand with its head. Often this barrage knocks the animal close to the ant lion's jaws once more.

Gripping its prey, the ant lion digs backward into the sand. Tufts of hair stick out from its body, anchoring the ant lion against the struggles of its prey. Once the ant lion has sucked out the body fluids, it flicks the dry carcass out of the pit.

Ant lions aren't stuck in the place they first hatch. They can move, plowing backward just beneath the surface, leaving crooked little furrows in the soil that look like doodles on paper; ant lions are sometimes called doodle bugs. They don't travel far but tend to congregate in areas protected from much direct sunlight, rain, or traffic by large animals. Look for their pits beside buildings, under the protection of overhanging eaves. Newly hatched larvae build small traps, whereas more mature ant lions dig pits that measure up to four inches across. Small or large, ant lions lie hidden in their simple homes, watching and waiting for their next meal.

3 At Home on Another

Struck by a car, a rabbit lay still by the road. It had stopped breathing and its body had begun to cool. Then, suddenly, the rabbit's fur seemed to twitch—on a leg, its side, its neck. Was it still alive?

No, the fur was moved by fleas and perhaps lice that had sensed that the rabbit was dead. It had been their home. The rabbit's blood had nourished them. Now these parasites were abandoning their host.

Very few living things are free of parasites, either outside (ectoparasites) or inside (endoparasites). Many parasites have parasites of their own, although it is not literally true, as Jonathan Swift wrote, that "a flea hath smaller fleas that on him prey, and these have smaller still to bite 'em." Fleas don't have fleas but do have such parasites as roundworms and immature tapeworms.

Some biologists believe that, counting sheer numbers of individuals, most animals on earth are parasites. Many thousands of insect species spend part of their lives on or in the bodies of other animals. Flatworms, nematodes, ticks, and mites are also important parasitic groups. Making a home on another animal is clearly a successful way of life. The host provides food and shelter, and parasites in most cases cause it little or no harm.

Some parasites are utterly dependent on their hosts. A tapeworm has no digestive system of its own and absorbs its food directly from its host's digestive tract. Other parasites need more than one host in order to complete their life cycle.

One small trematode fluke, for example, must live in three different organisms to become an adult. Its life cycle begins when an adult fluke lays eggs inside the intestines of a kingfisher, a fish-eating bird. The fluke eggs pass out of the bird with its body wastes. In water, microscopic forms called miracidia hatch from the eggs and swim about, seeking a snail. Within a snail miracidia develop into larvae, which leave their snail home and hunt for a fish. If successful they burrow beneath its scales or into its fins. There the small, white larvae form cysts, around which black pigment forms. The resulting black spots may be noticed by people when they catch minnows, sunfish, or other common freshwater fish.

The larvae stay on the fish and die when it dies, unless the fish is eaten by a kingfisher. If that happens the larvae develop into adults within the bird's digestive tract and produce eggs for a new generation.

Unless we are curious enough to investigate little black spots we see on the body of a fish, this is just one of many parasites we do not notice. There are, however, some parasites that live closer to home, perhaps in our homes, perhaps even on our bodies. The human body is a home for a variety of living things, including an estimated one hundred quadrillion bacterial cells. Many adults are also inhabited by follicle mites, which are almost invisible crea-

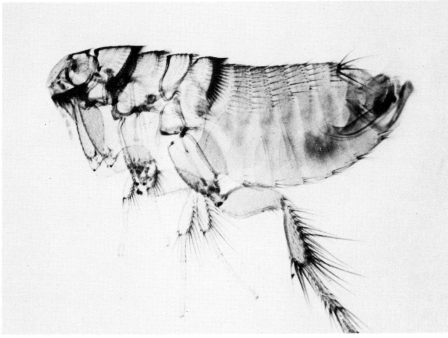

Visuals Unlimited (A.H. Benton)

Fleas are well-adapted for life in a thicket of hairs or feathers, with thin bodies and rows of spines (combs) on their heads that help them hold fast.

tures that spend their entire lives around the bases of hairs, especially those of the eyebrows and eyelashes. We almost never notice them.

Horses, monkeys, apes, and whales usually have no fleas. But Antarctic penguins do, and cottontail rabbits often have two species on their bodies—one on the head, the other on the back and sides. Fleas are well adapted for life in a home that resembles a thicket or forest. Their bodies are tall and thin and slip easily between hairs or feathers. On their heads are rows of thick spines, called combs, which enable them to cling to the hairs around them. Fleas that live on bats and birds have especially strong combs with which they hang on while their hosts fly. When you see a dog or cat scratching or biting at a flea, the insect probably

19

has a firm grip with its comb on several hairs, holding on for its life.

Most kinds of fleas spend only part of their adult lives on their favorite host animal. They visit warm-blooded animals in order to get meals of blood. Blade-like teeth cut the skin, then a muscular pump draws blood into the flea's digestive tract. The flea drinks until it is bloated. For every adult flea that is feeding or resting on a cat or dog there are usually six others resting on furniture or other places where the pet mammal rests.

Female fleas usually lay their eggs in dark places away from the host animal. White larvae hatch from the eggs in about a week. They feed on almost any organic matter, including hairs and the feces of adult fleas, which is partly digested blood. Each larva then spins a cocoon from which an adult flea emerges anytime from a week to a year later.

A single meal of blood can sustain an adult flea for several months. Usually fleas don't wait that long for a meal. They are skilled at finding hosts by detecting their odors and perhaps also sensing vibrations of animal movements. A few days after a biologist marked 270 rabbit fleas and let them go in a meadow, he found that nearly half of the fleas had found homes on three rabbits.

During its life a flea may have several homes, including more than one animal host. A louse usually has only one home—a bird or mammal on which it spends all life stages, from egg to adult. Lice do leave home, most commonly when they crawl from an adult host to take up residence on its young in a nest or den. But they soon die if removed from their animal home.

Lice are divided into two main groups—biting or chewing lice, which live on birds, and sucking lice, which are parasites of mammals, including humans. There are three types of human lice. Head lice are almost always found in the hair of the head. Body lice hide in clothing when not feeding on the human body. And crab lice live among the coarse hairs of the genital area.

These pests of people are only a few of many lice that have very specific homes. One species lives only in pelican pouches. Another bird, the glossy ibis, is home to four separate species of lice, each on a different part of the bird's body. The lice that live on an ibis's back and wings have very flat bodies and can move rapidly over feathers. These adaptations enable the lice to escape when the ibis grooms itself with its beak. In contrast, another kind of louse that lives on ibises has a more rounded body and moves slowly. These lice could be easily grabbed and crushed by the beak of an ibis but are safe where the bird cannot reach—on its head and most of its neck. That is where they live.

Bowling Green State University, Electron Microscopy Center

The head louse is one of three types of lice that live on humans. Other mammals may have as many as four species of lice on different parts of their bodies.

HOME

In the Antarctic, lice live on the hind flippers of elephant seals, the warmest place on their bodies. The lice burrow into sealskin with only the tips of their abdomens exposed. They need a temperature of about 77° F. to reproduce, and they experience this for only a few weeks a year, when the elephant seals come ashore. The seal mating season is also the time for mating and egg laying by their ectoparasites.

Lice are highly sensitive to changes in temperature. They abandon feverish animals and the cooling bodies of dead hosts. Some may survive by escaping in a remarkable way—hitching a ride on a fly to another home. Two biologists first reported this phenomenon in 1952. They examined a starling just after its death and found fifteen lice and one fly on its body. The fly was a parasite too, a hippoboscid fly that sucks blood from birds or mammals. They wrapped the dead bird in a cloth. Two hours later the biologists found that seven of the lice had attached themselves to the still-living fly.

Other biologists have since found that lice frequently ride on the abdomens of parasitic flies that visit starlings. Lice are airlifted from one live starling to another. Thus, if a hippoboscid fly is present when a starling dies and a louse can attach itself to the fly, it has a chance of reaching a new host.

The death of an animal does not end its role as a home for other organisms. As parasites die or flee, other creatures are attracted to a carcass as a food source and temporary home. In the wintertime, such scavengers as opossums have been found living inside the rib cages of dead bears or other large mammals.

In warmer seasons the scent of decaying flesh attracts such insects as blowflies and carrion beetles. Blowflies, which include the colorful greenbottle and bluebottle flies, lay their eggs in the flesh of dead birds and mammals. The eggs hatch quickly and the larvae, called maggots, feed on the carcass. In less than two weeks

22

they develop into pupae, the nonfeeding stage from which adult flies emerge.

Carrion beetles also appear soon after an animal dies. Both adults and larvae feed on its flesh. One type of carrion beetle, called the sexton or burying beetle, digs under the carcass of a small animal until it sinks into the ground. When the carcass is buried the female beetles lay eggs in little tunnels dug beside it. The adults wait for almost a week until the young hatch, then feed the larvae with partly digested meat. After two more weeks the larvae burrow into the carcass, feed some more, and then develop into pupae.

Burying beetles and bluebottle flies are scavengers, not parasites, but their lives illustrate that a living thing can provide a home for others both in life and in death.

Laurence Pringle

The odor of decay from a dead deer attracts carrion beetles, which make their home in the deer's body and reproduce there.

4 Animal Architects

Beyond the beaver lodge, a chimney swift skimmed over the pond and sipped water on the wing. Beneath the surface bluegill sunfish guarded their nests and caddis fly larvae inched along the bottom in their shelters made of plant stems. At the pond edge, mud dauber wasps grasped bits of mud and carried them off to build homes for a new generation of wasps.

Near a pond or even in a back yard you can often find homes built by several kinds of animals. Some are simple, like the pits that bluegills clear with the movements of their fins. Others are complex structures. Animal architects build with their teeth, beaks, claws, other body parts, and sometimes with special substances from their bodies. Their work has long been admired by human engineers and scientists.

Of all nonhuman builders, the beaver is unique because its dams can alter the environment over a large area and affect so many other living things, including people. Water impounded by a

By damming streams and flooding land, beavers destroy the habitat of some animals and create favorable environments for others.

beaver dam may flood roads, farmers' fields, orchards, and timber. Usually this isn't tolerated, and the beavers are captured and moved to a place where they may do little harm.

Wherever beavers erect dams in the wild, the environment is changed from a wooded valley floor to an open pond or series of ponds. Trees are felled for food by members of the beaver colony, but many more trees and shrubs drown because water keeps air from reaching their roots. Still standing, the trees provide homes for woodpeckers and tree swallows. And the pond itself is a home for certain animals that thrive in still waters—bullfrogs, salamanders, catfish, and numerous insect larvae.

Beavers do not always build dams. If food is available they live in lakes and rivers and dig burrows at the water's edge for shelter. But their dammed-up ponds often give beavers access to an abundant supply of such preferred foods as aspens. Where the terrain is flat they dig narrow canals that reach out to groves of tasty trees. It is easier and safer to float branches to the pond on canals than to drag them overland.

In a deep part of the pond beavers pile mud and stones and branches until the heap rises several feet above the surface. Then they hollow out two or more passages, with underwater entrances, that reach up to a den that lies above the water level. The mud and intertwined sticks at the top of the domed lodge are loose enough to allow air to pass in and out. On cold winter days you may see a little cloud of water vapor rising from the top of a beaver lodge—evidence that one or more beavers live comfortably within.

The phrase "busy as a beaver" suggests that beavers are year-round workaholics, but they lead rather easy lives once one or more dams and a lodge are built. In the summertime beavers usually eat easily obtained soft plant foods from the land and water. They swim near the dam, listen for the sound of leaking water, and repair an area where water is escaping. Biologists have found that it is the sound of water that stimulates beavers to make repairs. If a tape recording of running water is played at a certain section of a dam, beavers will try to fix a leak that does not exist.

The lodge is the center of beaver life. It is a safe refuge for daytime rest and the place where kits are born and live for the first two months of their lives. All winter long it is also a cozy shelter

Surrounded by water, the lodge (in background) is a nursery for beaver kits in the spring and a refuge for the beaver colony in all seasons.

that beavers leave only to swim out beneath the ice and pick a branch from their underwater food storage pile.

Beavers are difficult to observe. They are hidden away in winter and are active mostly at night in other seasons. Their lives still hold many mysteries. There is agreement among ecologists, however, that beaver home building has had a great effect on North American streams for many thousands of years. For example, when some ecologists recently looked for an undisturbed stream to study in the wild forests of eastern Canada, every creek and small river showed signs of having been altered by beavers. A colony's influence lasts long after it abandons part of a stream valley. Even after the dams wash away, grassy meadows remain and flourish for decades until the forest closes in.

Among the animals affected by beavers are the larvae of certain caddis flies. Net-spinning species, described in the second chapter, can only survive where a current brings food to their webs. They disappear from parts of streams that beavers change into broad ponds. There are other kinds of home-building caddis flies, however, including species that thrive in the quiet waters of beaver ponds.

Soon after hatching a caddis fly larva begins to build a protective shelter from bits of material cemented together with silk-like threads produced by its saliva glands. Using its legs and jaws it picks up building material and sticks it onto a silken foundation. In still waters the larva uses lightweight parts of plant stems or leaves. Stems may be cut to a specific length. Where a current flows the larva builds with heavier objects such as sand grains, small pebbles, and little snail shells.

Some of the protective cases look haphazard whereas others resemble neat little log cabins or fine masonry. Only a few kinds of larvae can be identified by the structure of their cases. In general the insects build with whatever materials are available. A caddis fly

Sand grains cemented together with silk make mobile homes for these caddis fly larvae. In a stronger current they would build with heavier materials.

home might include gold nuggets if those of the right size and weight are present on a stream bottom. In a laboratory tank a caddis fly larva made its home of gold dust—the only building material supplied by its keeper.

Near shore you may see odd-looking caddis fly structures moving about. At one end of these camouflage suits the larva's head and front legs protrude. If you touch it the larva withdraws into its shelter and grips the inside tightly with hooks at the end of its abdomen.

Caddis fly larvae feed on living or dead plant material. As they grow in size they enlarge their mobile homes. When a larva is fully grown it fastens its home to a sturdy object and spins a door for the front opening, leaving a slit to admit water, from which the insect absorbs vital oxygen. It becomes a pupa and within its pupal skin develops into a winged adult that wriggles out of its home, rises to the surface, and takes to the air. Grayish-brown adult caddis flies resemble moths or butterflies. They live for only a few weeks. Before they die, females that have mated lay eggs at the water's edge, or, in many species, actually creep back underwater and lay eggs on the undersides of stones.

Some freshwater fishes are home builders, although the adult fishes make shelters for their eggs or young, not for themselves. Many fishes clear a pit on the bottom of a stream, pond, or lake. Spawning occurs on this nest and in some species the male fish guards the fertilized eggs.

Some stream fishes pile stones into a sort of nest. River chubs, for instance, can lift in their mouths stones that are twice as big as their heads. They push even larger stones along the bottom with their snouts. In a few days one six-inch-long male river chub can move several thousand stones and pebbles and build a mound almost a foot high and three feet across. When the male spawns with a female chub over the nest, the fertilized eggs settle into crevices among the stones. The height of the pile above the streambed ensures that water will flow among the stones and bathe the eggs in oxygen.

More complex nests are built by sticklebacks—a group of small fishes, two to four inches long, that includes both freshwater and saltwater species. (Some species are at home in both freshwater and marine habitat.) In its bright mating colors—blue eyes and red underside—each male stickleback searches for a nesting site, ideally one with a sandy bottom and nearby water plants.

After picking a spot, the stickleback digs a shallow pit, then collects leaves and stems from the surroundings. A loose pile of this material is deposited over the pit. The male swims repeatedly across the nest, secreting from his kidneys a sticky substance that glues the stuff together. He spits onto the unkempt pile mouthfuls of sand grains, which add support. Then he squirms into the pile and creates a hollow within. Pushing the ceiling upward, the fish enlarges the chamber. Finally he pokes another opening—a back door—and the nest is ready.

With special swimming motions the male lures a female to enter, then prods her tail, causing her to release eggs in the nest. She slips out the back door; he enters by the front and fertilizes the eggs. In this manner, a male stickleback may entice several females to spawn until the nest contains several hundred eggs. Then he guards the nest, chasing away all intruders, including female sticklebacks.

Beating his fins at the entrance, the male stickleback forces water over the eggs. He mends the nest if necessary, and pokes holes in it if the eggs seem to need better circulation of water. He also guards the young when they hatch and leave the nest. Usually they stay close to the nest in a compact school until, after a few weeks, they leave their home area and their father.

Among alligators and crocodiles it is females that build nests. On early June nights they crawl from the water and make a mound of earth and vegetation. They haul huge mouthfuls of rushes, mud, roots, and partly decayed plants from the water and shore and use both front and hind legs to shape the material. A complete nest mound is usually three feet high and six feet across.

The alligator completes the nest by digging a foot-deep pit in the center of the mound. There she lays from twenty to fifty-five eggs, positioning each one in the nest with a hind foot. Then she grasps nesting material and gently covers the eggs. She also packs the mound down by crawling across it several times. In the following weeks she splashes water on the nest with her tail or voids water on it from her own body. This aids the decay of the vegeta-

Female alligators carry mouthfuls of mud and vegetation in order to shape a nest in which their eggs will hatch, aided by heat given off by decaying plants.

tion in the mound. The process of decay provides the heat needed to incubate the eggs.

The eggs hatch in about two months. During this time the female stays near by, ready to charge and threaten any intruders. When baby alligators hatch they make a high-pitched *erk* sound, to which the mother responds. She comes to the nest and digs the babies out. She carries some to the water in her jaws and makes grunting sounds that lure the others to follow. This maternal care is crucial to the survival of the young. If their mother is killed and cannot help them emerge, they starve to death. Their nest becomes their grave.

Like alligators, most birds build nests that are not year-round homes but that protect eggs and young. Some birds, in fact, build nests similar to those of alligators. The brush turkey of eastern Australia, for example, makes a large mound in which heat from decaying vegetation incubates the eggs. While some birds make intricately woven nests, most build rather simple structures and some species, such as the killdeer, just lay their eggs on bare ground. Most nests are abandoned after the young have flown, although nesting cavities in trees and birdhouses may be used year after year (but not necessarily by the same individual birds or species). Large birds that usually nest in tall trees, such as eagles, ospreys, and great blue herons, may use the same nest year after year, adding fresh material each spring.

Pigeons and doves build especially scanty nests in which they usually lay just two eggs. Their nest-making skills are described in an old English nursery rhyme:

> Coo, coo, coo
> Me and my poor two
> Two sticks across
> And a little bit of moss
> And it will do, do, do.

Eggs sometimes roll right out of a dove nest. Most birds make cup-shaped nests that enclose the eggs and young. Coarse materials make up the foundation and outer walls; fine materials line the interior. The nests of some species can be identified by materials they always include, for example, a lining of thistledown in goldfinch nests and of grapevine bark in catbird nests. Crested

Great blue herons return to the same nesting rookery year after year and often add sticks to nests used by previous generations of herons.

Laurence Pringle

A slight depression in the ground, often with no lining, is the nesting site for killdeer, which sometimes nest on the flat roofs of buildings.

flycatchers, which nest in tree cavities, usually include a shed snakeskin in their nests. They also use substitutes that resemble snakeskins—onionskins or part of a tattered plastic bag.

No North American birds make nests as finely crafted as the weaverbirds of Africa and southern Asia, which are among the masters of all animal builders. Using interlocking loops, spiral coils, and such knots as the half hitch and slip knot, a male weaverbird makes a nest of grasses or palm fronds that must be

35

inspected and approved by a female. If no female accepts the nest within a week or so, he takes it apart and tries again in the same place. The male takes this possibility into account—as he builds he does not pull knots tight, since he may soon be undoing them. Each new home is usually an improvement over the last, and eventually a female shows her approval by bringing bits of soft materials with which she lines the nest where she will lay her eggs.

In North America the only close relative of these weaverbirds is the English or house sparrow, introduced from Europe. It shows no great weaving skills in its bulky, loose nests. Orioles, hummingbirds, and swifts are among the native North American birds that build exceptional nests. Finely woven gourd-shaped nests of northern orioles hang from the tips of drooping tree branches, well out of reach of most predators. Ruby-throated hummingbird nests, only one and one-half inches across, often have an outer surface of gray lichens and resemble a bump on a tree branch. Silk from spider webs is a favorite building material of hummingbirds.

Before there were chimneys in North America there were birds we call chimney swifts, which then nested in hollow trees. They still nest and roost in such shelters in wilderness areas of the eastern United States, as do Vaux's swifts west of the Rockies. Swifts do not land to collect nesting materials but break off twigs with their feet while flying. The twigs are glued with sticky saliva to form a shallow bracket on the inside surface of a chimney or hollow tree. (In caves of the Far East, swifts make half-cup-shaped nests entirely of saliva. These nests are made into bird's nest soup and other delicacies. In Hong Kong a bowl of bird's nest soup costs from $14 to $38, and up to a thousand dollars may be charged for a pound of top-quality nests.) Even when not raising young, chimney swifts and Vaux's swifts rest within chimneys or hollow trees, both in North America and in their winter range in South America.

The sticky saliva that holds twigs together can be seen in this chimney swift nest built on a barn wall.

Richard B. Fischer

A pair of adult swifts rest at their nest attached to a rug hung vertically in a barn.

Most species of birds require special shelter only during the reproductive season, to help protect the new generation. There are exceptions: woodpeckers and other hole-nesting birds also roost year around inside such shelters; cactus wrens build spherical nests that are sleeping quarters in all seasons. Even the young wrens build their own winter nests. Most birds, however, seek a simple home that protects them while asleep, in the shelter of a tree, shrub, or other vegetation.

5 Community Homes

Ants, termites, paper wasps, bumblebees, and honeybees cannot survive for long as individuals. They are social insects and live in colonies. For many centuries their lives have intrigued other social creatures, humans. The more we learn about social insects, the more complex their lives seem. We now know that among honeybees, for example, worker bees may be assigned one of a dozen or more jobs that help their colony function. These include: undertaker (removing dead bees from the hive), water collector (bringing in water to maintain desirable humidity), and fanner (beating wings to circulate air through the hive).

The behavior, reproduction, and chemical signals of social insects have been the subject of countless studies, reports, and books. Here we will focus on just one vital part of the lives of social insects—home building.

Some of the most remarkable homes of social insects occur in the tropics, where termites build mounds composed of several

Collecting food is just one of a dozen or more jobs performed by worker honeybees that help sustain their home colony.

tons of soil. One African nest mound was broken up and yielded enough clay to make 450,000 bricks. In some areas termite mounds dominate the landscape, rising more than twenty feet above the plains. The outer surface of these mounds is compact and strong, protecting the occupants from heat and predators. Many termites use their body wastes as a binder or glue to hold pellets of soil together.

Climate control is vital for termites. Maintaining high humidity and a certain temperature ensures development of the young and

Australia's compass termites detect the earth's magnetic field and align their huge mounds with narrow, pointed sides facing north and south, broad sides facing east and west.

storage or even production of food. (Some species feed on fungi grown on a mulch of vegetation within their home.) Desert termites dig shafts more than a hundred feet deep in order to find water for the colony. In some species, worker termites carry wet clay pellets up to the nest interior; this helps maintain needed moisture in the air. A suitable interior microclimate is also maintained by systems of chambers, ducts, and sometimes chimney-like structures. In Australia, so-called compass termites build slender mounds whose broad sides face east and west rather than north and south. This reduces exposure of the mound to the strong midday rays of the sun.

The actual building behavior of termites is fascinating to watch. In Ceylon a biologist named Karl Escherich deliberately broke a hole in a termite colony's covered runway that led up a tree trunk. He saw some termites flee into the undamaged tunnel. Then, after a few minutes, a soldier termite appeared and carefully inspected the damage. It left and soon several soldiers arrived and took up positions at the top and bottom of the opening.

Workers appeared and began to repair the damage. A worker would deposit excrement on the broken edge of the tunnel, then another worker would press a soil particle into the excrement. The body waste served as a kind of mortar for soil "bricks." And so, brick by brick, in a few hours the tunnel wall was repaired and sealed to the outside world.

You can watch a similar process in North America, where the most common termites also build and repair covered runways. In general these termites make rather primitive homes compared to the work of their tropical relatives. Their food is cellulose, a major component of wood. From nests deep underground they tunnel through the soil and feed on roots, stumps, logs lying on the surface, and wooden parts of homes and other buildings. Often they build a protective runway, about a quarter inch in diameter, that

Laurence Pringle

Termites roam far from home, sometimes to the attics of houses, but must avoid exposure to light and return daily to their underground nest.

reaches from the ground, up a concrete foundation wall, and into a wooden board. Made of soil, bits of wood, and excrement, these runways enable termites to reach a supply of wood while maintaining the dark, humid environment they need.

Each day termites carry wood back to their underground chambers. They also must return to get water from belowground or they will die. Their secret underground society may go undetected for years as they chew through wood and even books and piles of newspapers. They may reach the attic of a two-story house in their quest for cellulose. If they accidentally break through the outer surface of a beam or other piece of wood they quickly plug the hole. Termite colonies are usually discovered in the spring, the season when swarms of winged nymphs break out in the open and flutter weakly away, seeking a site for a new colony.

Ants also have a winged reproductive form, and many people believe that termite nymphs are "flying ants." But swarming termites soon land and shed their wings before digging underground. Swarming ants do not shed their wings.

Some ants, including the large, shiny black carpenter ants, also make their homes in wood. They do not eat wood but just chew it and spit out the sawdust as they cut tunnels and chambers in which to live. Carpenter ants prefer partly decayed wood that is easy to tunnel in but sometimes build homes in solid wood. Here again they chew away the softer parts, formed in the springtime, and leave the hard, compact wood that was laid down in past summers. Carpenter ants take nectar from flowers and collect seeds and a variety of other foods. When they encounter termites, as they often do, they eat them.

Most ants nest underground. Tip back a good-sized rock and you will probably uncover some of the living chambers of an ant colony. Workers scurry off with larvae or pupae in their jaws, carrying them to safety.

Some ants build hills of soil above their underground nest. The hills of small species rise only an inch or two above the surface. Other anthills rise several feet in the air. Workers carry twigs, grass stems, and other materials in from the surroundings. They use small objects to line inside chambers and tunnels. Larger items are left on the slopes of the hill where they are gradually covered by soil and give support to the home.

Work on the anthill never ends. A scientist once sprayed a blue dye on a hill occupied by red wood ants. Four days later the hill surface was brown again. The blue soil particles were found three to four inches below the surface. A month later the scientist found the blue particles scattered at a depth of sixteen inches. As more time passed, however, the blue particles began to appear on the surface again. The movement of this marked soil was the result of

45

ants carrying soil from the lowest parts of their nest to deposit it on the outer surface. This helps keep the interior of their home from becoming too moist and prevents mold from forming.

Ants also affect their home microclimate by basking in the sun and then going underground, warming the air there. They open or close ventilation holes at the top of their mounds, depending on whether the colony needs to gain or lose heat. They also close all entrances to the anthill on especially cool summer days or nights. At such times the actual structure of an anthill may make heat available to its occupants. By rising above the surface an anthill intercepts more sunrays in the morning and late afternoon than a flat area would. This is especially important for ants that live in cool temperate climates.

Whereas all ants and termites live year around in colonies, many bees and wasps lead solitary lives and make homes only for reproductive purposes. Paper wasps and hornets are social insects, however, and are familiar because the nests of some species are frequently noticed by people. The term hornet is usually applied to the white-faced hornet, which builds large paper nests in shrubs or trees and sometimes on buildings. Mated females remain dormant beneath tree bark or a similar refuge in the winter, then awaken in the spring and hunt for a home site. Each female will be the queen of a new hornet colony.

With her mandibles the hornet shaves off particles from trees, boards, and other sources of weathered wood. Mixed with saliva, the wood particles become a pulp that dries quickly to form a tough paper. With little strips of this material she makes the first cells in which she lays eggs for a new generation of hornets. The cells are enclosed in a few thin paper layers. At this point the nest is about the size of a golfball, with an entrance hole at the bottom.

When the first batch of worker hornets emerge they take over the jobs of cell building and adding new layers of paper that sur-

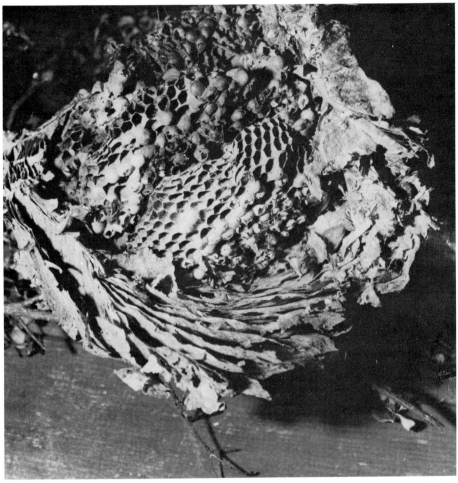

When paper walls of a hornet's nest are torn away, several horizontal layers of combs where young develop are revealed.

round and protect the cells. As more workers appear the hornet home grows outward and downward, with several layers of cell-bearing combs stacked horizontally. By late summer the hornet colony may include several hundred workers and the paper nest may be the size of a basketball.

A hornet community includes workers that help maintain a temperature of about 86° F. near the cells where new hornets are developing. When they sense that the temperature is too low they exercise vigorously, contracting and stretching their abdomens and giving off increased heat from their bodies. If they sense that the temperature is too high they carry in water and wet the cells.

As summer ends, new queens and males (drones) emerge from cells and leave their home and mate. The males die but the queens seek shelter for the winter. In the meantime, the hornet community breaks down. The old queen dies, and the remaining workers may eat the larvae that remain in the cells. By the first frost all of the workers die. Then the paper nest, once a bustling center of hornet life, hangs silent and empty. It is not used again.

The lives of bumblebees resemble those of white-faced hornets. A large bumblebee we see in the spring is a queen that mated the previous summer. Like a hornet queen, she is seeking a home site. Also like a hornet queen, she is responsible for beginning the nest and producing a group of workers before she gets help for further construction and food getting.

Rather than make paper, however, bumblebees (and honeybees) produce flakes of wax from abdominal skin glands. This wax, kneaded with pollen grains, is the basic building material for the walls of rounded cells in which larvae develop or honey is stored. Reserves of honey enable bumblebees to survive rainy days when food gathering is difficult, but they are not sufficient to last all winter. So the workers and drones die, the nest is abandoned, and future generations of bumblebees depend on the success of young queens finding shelter where they will spend the winter.

Bumblebee nests are often built underground, in an old mousehole or similar burrow. The waxen cells are rather coarsely made and are often protected by a covering of moss. These nests are far from the best built in the bee family, which includes more than 20,000 species. Most species are solitary, not social. Some cut

Bernd Heinrich

Inside an abandoned mouse nest, a newly-emerged worker bumblebee sips from a honeypot. By summer's end, a bumblebee colony has many honeypots and workers.

parts of leaves and fasten them together to form nests; others make cells from a mortar of sand and saliva. In his book *Animal Architects,* Karl von Frisch wrote, "The homes of some bees look almost as if they were the work of architects simply bursting with ideas and using all kinds of techniques, with the all-important difference that the bees, guided by their marvelous instincts, can do it all without thinking."

People learned to keep honeybees in artificial homes at least 5,000 years ago. Long before humans existed the bees nested in tree hollows, rock crevices, and similar shelters. Colonies of wild honeybees still live in such places. Whether wild or domesticated, honeybees usually occupy an existing outer structure in which they build elaborate and finely crafted waxen honeycombs.

A colony may number as many as 60,000 bees and is capable of storing large amounts of honey. This enables the entire colony to survive over winter in temperate regions. The bees cluster together and occasionally sip honey, burning food energy and resisting freezing temperatures. A queen may live several years. When she dies a new young queen takes her place, so a honeybee community can go on for many years in the same shelter.

Honeybee combs hang vertically. Some cells store honey or pollen, others are brood cells where new bees develop. A few very large cells with rounded walls are reserved for rearing some spare

Troy H. Fore, Jr.

Combs of honeybees hang vertically, and each hexagonal cell is tilted slightly upward; this keeps honey from dripping out before the cell is sealed with wax.

queens. All other cells are shaped like hexagons and are tilted slightly upward at an angle of 13 degrees from the horizontal. This keeps the thick honey from running out of the cell before it is sealed with a wax lid. The six-sided cell shape is the ideal design for strength and also for conserving space and building material.

Honeybee workers cluster together when building. The heat given off from their bodies helps maintain a temperature of 95° F., which is needed for their wax glands to produce. The wax is kneaded with saliva, then molded into place. The cells they make are quite uniform, with walls that are about three-hundredths of an inch (.073 millimeters) thick. Sense organs at the tips of a worker bee's antennae enable her to gauge the thickness of cell walls. She presses her antennae against a section of wall, and the sense organs measure the movement this causes. The bee then knows whether the wall is correct as is, needs more wax, or needs wax removed. When their antennae tips are removed, honeybee workers make irregular cell walls with holes and thin and thick areas.

In addition to their well-known beeswax, honeybees use another building material, one not produced from their own bodies. It is called propolis, or bee's glue. Workers collect it outdoors by chewing sticky resins from tree buds, then carrying it home on their hind legs. Propolis is used mainly for filling in gaps and cracks, especially in early autumn when cold nights reveal where chilly drafts enter the nest.

Like many a human family, honeybees caulk and cover the places where precious heat escapes. This reduces their energy cost and provides a more comfortable home in winter.

6 No Place Like Home

A summer chorus of cicadas is hard to ignore. Whirring, buzzing cicada sounds can be so loud that people outdoors can hardly carry on a conversation. They complain about the "locusts," as cicadas are commonly but mistakenly named (locusts are short-antennaed grasshoppers).

Like most animals, cicadas have more than one home during their life. Those loud summer sounds announce the presence of adult male cicadas high in trees. Females respond to the mating call and find mates in the sunny treetops. Both males and females live only a few weeks. Before dying the females cut slits in branches and lay eggs in them. The eggs develop for about two months until tiny wingless cicada nymphs emerge. They leap into the air, land on the ground, and burrow in.

Some species of cicada mature in a year or a few years. There are a few species in the eastern United States, however, that spend an extraordinary time belowground as nymphs. Some cicadas with

After emerging from its nymphal skin, an adult male cicada begins to rasp its summer song. This species matures in two years; others have thirteen-year or seventeen-year life cycles.

a thirteen-year life cycle inhabit the South and Midwest, and others with a seventeen-year life-span live in the Northeast.

Underground the nymphs suck fluids from rootlets. As they grow they molt five times, shedding old skins, emerging with new, roomier ones. No one understands how these insects "know" when to come to the surface after thirteen or seventeen years in the soil. When the time arrives, at dusk on a summer evening, they dig free of their earthen homes by the thousands. Each nymph climbs up a nearby vertical object, usually a tree. As the nymph clings there its skin splits open down the back and an adult cicada wriggles out. A seventeen-year cicada's underground home is a safe haven compared with its habitat during its brief adult life. Blue jays and other large birds easily find and catch the big insects.

In contrast to the hidden-away life of cicada nymphs, the homes of froghopper nymphs are aboveground and in plain sight. Froghoppers are related to cicadas. Adult froghoppers are small, inconspicuous insects that suck fluids from plants. They seldom fly, usually hopping from plant to plant.

Froghoppers have another common name—spittlebugs—which stems from the unusual homes of their nymphs. They live in masses of white froth that looks like spittle. People used to believe they had found frog or bird spit when they saw these blobs of glistening froth on plants.

Each froghopper nymph makes its own foam home. It clings head-down to a plant and sinks its mouthparts deep into the tissues. Sap flows into the insect's body. In fact, much of it moves right through and out the end of the nymph's abdomen and then down over its body in a glistening sheath. Then the nymph is ready to make bubbles.

It lifts the tip of its abdomen out of the fluid and takes air into a special chamber. Then it lowers its abdomen and forces the air out into the fluid. A bubble forms. The nymph can bob its abdomen up and down once a second, producing sixty bubbles a minute, although it usually pauses for rest.

As the mass of bubbles grows in size, gravity pulls it down over the nymph's body and beyond its head. Within twenty minutes

An insect nymph, the spittlebug, lives within a home of bubbles on a plant stem. Spittlebugs make this foam from plant sap, air, and a waxy substance.

the nymph is completely hidden in a bubble cluster that protects it from predators. Unlike ordinary soap bubbles, these do not break easily. As plant sap passes through a nymph's body a waxy substance is added, which strengthens the bubbles. The froth stays intact for a week or more. Then the nymph makes a new home.

Male dragonflies stake out a new territory each day. They try to mate with females that fly into their space, and chase other males away.

nest in holes they dig in sand or gravel banks, the territory is a few square inches around their burrow entrance. At the opposite extreme, a golden eagle's territory may encompass more than thirty square miles.

Most birds defend a territory only during the reproductive season. At its conclusion, robins and blackbirds begin to forage and travel in flocks. The record for short-lived territorial holdings belongs to dragonflies and damselflies. The males establish a new territory each day. They defend part of a pond against other males and try to mate with females that enter their space. Each morning, however, they stake out a different territory. In contrast, a pack of wolves may keep the same territory for decades. Individual wolves die and are replaced but the basic boundaries often stay the same.

On rare occasions animals engage in deadly combat over territory. This occurred during the early 1970s in northern Minnesota when an extreme food shortage caused some packs of wolves to trespass onto the territories of others. Some wolves actually died of their wounds. Under normal conditions wolf packs respect each

Laurence Pringle

Generations of wolves may defend the same territory over a span of many years, by howling, scent-marking, and—rarely—by actual combat with other wolves.

59

other's territorial borders. Wolves are ancestors of dogs, and you may have seen a dog defend its home territory with barks, growls, threatening facial expressions, and—if necessary—direct attack on an intruder.

The drive to establish a home and to keep it is very strong. Dogs, wolves, and many other animals have shown great determination to return home when released far away. Migratory birds travel thousands of miles to a winter range, then return to the same neighborhood and even to the same suburban lot or birdhouse where they nested the previous year. One of the most remarkable examples of a bird's homing instinct occurred in the 1950s, when a seabird called the Manx shearwater was taken from its nest on the coast of Wales. The bird was let go at Boston, Massachusetts. Twelve days later the shearwater reached its nest, having flown 3,050 miles across the Atlantic.

The homing instinct of salmon brings them back to the stream where they were born. Returning from an ocean journey that spans several years and thousands of miles, the salmon detect a particular scent carried downstream from their original home, which usually lies many miles inland. Driven by the urge to reproduce in the same waters, the salmon battle upstream, often leaping several feet in the air in an effort to pass steep rapids and waterfalls. But salmon cannot leap over giant dams built to produce hydroelectric power, and such dams have prevented salmon from reaching their traditional spawning areas. Most of these salmon populations no longer exist. People unintentionally wiped them out by blocking access to their special reproductive home.

Many other animals are especially vulnerable during their breeding season. A threat to nests, dens, territories, or other kinds of homes can threaten the survival of whole populations or an entire species. This is the case of eastern bluebirds, once a common species east of the Great Plains in the United States. Their numbers have declined by about 90 percent since the 1930s. Suburban development has destroyed some of their habitat; so has intensive farming that leaves few trees or fencerows near open fields. Most damaging, however, is aggressive competition from starlings and English sparrows for nesting sites: abandoned woodpecker holes in dead trees and wooden fence posts.

Fortunately, there are ways to reduce this competition. Bluebirds nest readily in birdhouses, and houses with entrances no larger than one and a half inches in diameter will admit bluebirds but not starlings. Houses set well away from buildings and no more than five feet off the ground attract bluebirds but not English sparrows. Using this knowledge, people in some areas have set up hundreds of birdhouses and have helped local bluebird populations rebound.

In the case of bluebirds, action by one person or a few individuals can have a dramatic effect on bird numbers. But many birdwatchers and other people in North America feel powerless to help scores of other songbirds whose populations seem to be declining. These birds, which include wood warblers, tanagers, and flycatchers, have abundant nesting habitats in the United States and Canada but are losing ground in their winter ranges. Their homes in Latin America are being destroyed as tropical forests are cleared at an alarming rate. Barn swallows seem to benefit from this process but many other migratory species find their traditional winter homes disappearing.

Monarch butterflies are also most vulnerable in the wintertime. They reproduce successfully over most of the United States and southern Canada. Eggs are laid on common milkweed plants, and the colorful larvae feed on milkweed leaves. The orange and black adults are migratory and fly to winter resting sites. West of the Rocky Mountains about ten million monarchs head for winter roosts along the California coast. Seven of forty-five known sites

BLUEBIRD NESTING BOX

This diagram shows how to cut lumber (¾-inch pine, cedar, or redwood) to make the parts of a nesting box for bluebirds. The predator guard (shown in the drawing of completed house but not in photograph) makes it difficult for raccoons and other predators to reach into the house for eggs or nestlings. The entrance hole must be exactly 1½ inches in diameter to admit bluebirds but not starlings. The ¼-space between front and roof aids ventilation. Bluebird houses should be cleaned in the spring and between nestings in the summer, so a way must be provided to open the top, front, or a side. The house shown here has a front that pivots near the top on two nails. Further information on helping eastern, western, and mountain bluebirds can be obtained from the North American Bluebird Society, Box 6295, Silver Spring, Maryland 20906.

Laurence Pringle

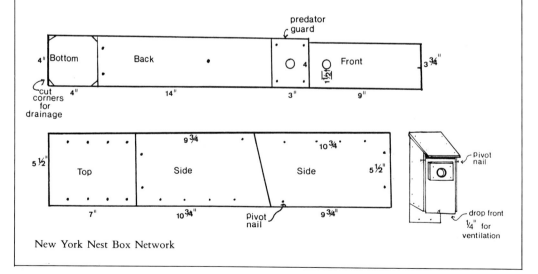

New York Nest Box Network

Individual monarch butterflies are scattered over a vast range in the summertime but are highly concentrated and vulnerable in their winter homes.

have already been destroyed by housing or business developments.

East of the Rockies an estimated one hundred million monarchs also migrate. They fly to central Mexico and gather at about twenty five- to seven-acre patches of fir forests on south-facing mountain slopes. Dense stands of firs protect the butterflies, and the climate is ideal for their relatively inactive lives. The butterflies must conserve energy in order to survive cool nights and to make the long flight home.

Destruction of these winter homes could wipe out all of the eastern monarchs. Some roosting sites have already been harmed

Without a larger shell to occupy, a growing hermit crab may eventually have no home at all and be easily killed by a predator.

by logging. In 1986 the Mexican government prohibited logging and development at twenty roosting sites. Landowners are being encouraged to preserve the butterflys' winter homes and to profit from the insects by attracting tourists to the spectacle of millions of resting monarchs. There is hope for the butterflies, but their dense concentration in small areas puts them at great risk.

Clearly, each home in an animal's life is vital to its survival. The island of Bermuda provides another example: large hermit crabs that live along its shores. Like all hermit crabs, these crustaceans occupy empty snail shells. Hermit crab bodies are adapted to fit into these borrowed homes. Their abdomens are curved and fit neatly into spiral shells, and their hind legs have become hook-like and hold the crab firmly within. As the crabs grow, however, they must find larger shells to accommodate their larger selves. Hermit crabs frequently investigate empty shells, feeling them, trying them on for size.

On Bermuda, Harvard biologist Stephen Jay Gould noticed large hermit crabs that had stuffed themselves partway into small shells. Their mobile homes offered them little protection from predators. Eventually he saw several hermit crabs in big shells that fit them well, but each of these shells was a fossil. Gould learned that the large snails of Bermuda are extinct, killed by people for food, and a small number of fossils are all that remain on the island. Each year some of these precious shelters break apart in the waves; the supply of proper homes for the large crabs diminishes. Without adequate protection, the hermit crabs may also face extinction on Bermuda.

The hermit crab's plight shows once more that all of an animal's homes can be matters of life and death. It also brings to mind that old saying, "There's no place like home." People say that to express appreciation for the warmth and security of home, but the words can have another meaning. What happens to an animal when it finds "there's no place like home"—no place remaining that is like the snail shell or nesting site it needs for life?

Anyone who cares about saving the earth's rich variety of animal life must also care about all of the diverse places that are animal homes.

Further Reading

Able, Kenneth, *et al.* "Burrow Construction and Behavior of the Tilefish, *Lopholatilus chamaeleonticeps,* in Hudson Submarine Canyon." *Environmental Biology of Fishes,* vol. 7, no. 3 (1982): 199–205.

Alstad, D.N. "Current Speed and Filtration Rate Link Caddisfly Phylogeny and Distribution Patterns on a Stream Gradient." *Science* vol. 216, no. 4545, (April 30, 1982): 533–34.

Askew, R. R. *Parasitic Insects.* New York: American Elsevier, 1971.

Ching, Thomas. *General Parasitology.* New York: Academic Press, 1973.

Collias, Nicholas and Elsie. *Nest Building and Bird Behavior.* Princeton, N.J.: Princeton University Press, 1984.

Costello, David. *The World of the Prairie Dog.* New York: J. B. Lippincott, 1970.

Eisner, Thomas, and Nowicki, Stephen. "Spider Web Protection Through Visual Advertisement: Role of the Stabilimentum." *Science* vol. 219, no. 4581, (January 14, 1983): 185–87.

Evans, Howard Ensign. *The Pleasures of Entomology: Portraits of Insects and the People Who Study Them.* Washington, D.C.: Smithsonian Institution Press, 1985.

———. *Wasp Farm: A Scientist's Account of the Remarkable Lives of Wasps.* Garden City, N.Y.: Natural History Press, 1963.

FURTHER READING

Gould, Stephen Jay. "Nature's Odd Couples." *Natural History* vol. 85, no. 1, (January 1978): 38–41.

Gunderson, Harvey. "Under and Around a Prairie Dog Town." *Natural History* vol. 85, no. 10, (October 1978): 56–67.

Hancocks, David. *Master Builders of the Animal World.* New York: Harper & Row, 1973.

Heinrich, Bernd. *Bumblebee Economics.* Cambridge, Mass.: Harvard University Press, 1979.

Hopf, Alice. *Whose House Is It?* New York: Dodd, Mead & Co., 1980.

Hutchins, Ross. *The Ant Realm.* New York: Dodd, Mead & Co., 1967.

Hynes, H.B.N. *The Ecology of Running Water.* Toronto: University of Toronto Press, 1970.

Marples, Mary. "Life on the Human Skin." *Scientific American* vol. 220, no. 1, (January 1969): 108–15.

Marshall, Adrian. *The Ecology of Ectoparasitic Insects.* New York: Academic Press, 1981.

Norman, Colin. "Mexico Acts to Protect Overwintering Monarchs." *Science* vol. 233, no. 4770, (September 19, 1986): 1252–53.

Ordish, George. *The Living American House: The 350-Year Story of a Home, an Ecological History.* New York: William Morrow & Co., 1981.

Patent, Dorothy Hinshaw. *The Lives of Spiders.* New York: Holiday House, 1980.

Prestwich, Glenn. "Dwellers in the Dark: Termites." *National Geographic* vol. 162, no. 4, (April 1978): 532–47.

Pringle, Laurence. *Frost Hollows and Other Microclimates.* New York: William Morrow & Co., 1981.

Simon, Chris. "Debut of the Seventeen-Year-Old Cicada." *Natural History* vol. 86, no. 5, (May 1979): 38–44.

Teal, John and Mildred. *Life and Death of the Salt Marsh.* New York: Ballantine Books, 1969.

Topoff, Howard. "The Pit and the Antlion." *Natural History* vol. 84, no. 4, (April 1977): 64–71.

von Frisch, Karl. *Animal Architecture.* New York: Harcourt Brace Jovanovich, 1974.

Welty, Joel. *The Life of Birds.* Philadelphia: W. B. Saunders, 1975.

Wilson, Edward. *Sociobiology.* Cambridge, Mass.: Harvard University Press, 1975.

Index

INDEX

15